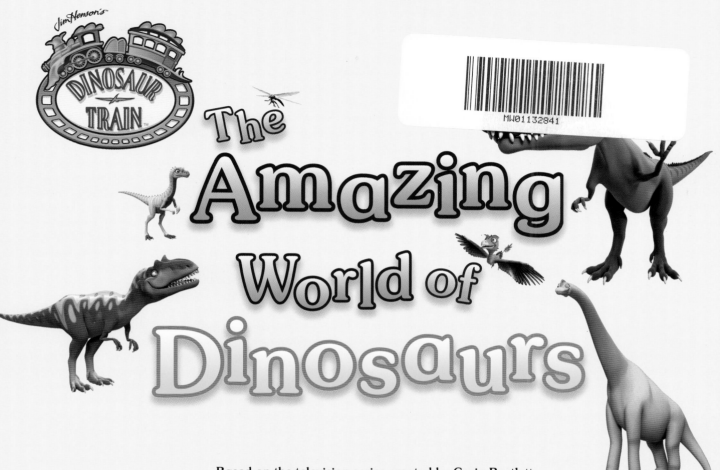

The Amazing World of Dinosaurs

Based on the television series created by Craig Bartlett

Grosset & Dunlap
An Imprint of Penguin Group (USA) Inc.

ISBN 978-0-448-46274-5   10 9 8 7 6 5 4 3 2 1

WELCOME ABOARD THE DINOSAUR TRAIN!

Hello! I'm Mr. Conductor. Let's take a trip back in time to learn about the extraordinary world of dinosaurs.

I am a Troodon, one of the most intelligent dinosaurs. I know lots of information about every kind of dinosaur.

WHAT IS A DINOSAUR?

That's a very good question! The word *dinosaur* means "terrible reptile" because dinosaurs were reptiles, like lizards! Other reptiles include crocodiles, snakes, turtles, and even birds!

Let's look at our friend Trudy Triceratops. Like many reptiles, her skin is scaly and she was born from an egg.

scales + egg = reptile!

DEFINITELY DIFFERENT!

There is another difference between dinosaurs and the rest of the reptile family. Some dinosaurs were warm-blooded, just like you! Usually reptiles are cold-blooded, which means they use the heat of the sun to keep themselves warm and go underground in the winter to hibernate. But many dinosaurs could remain active all year long.

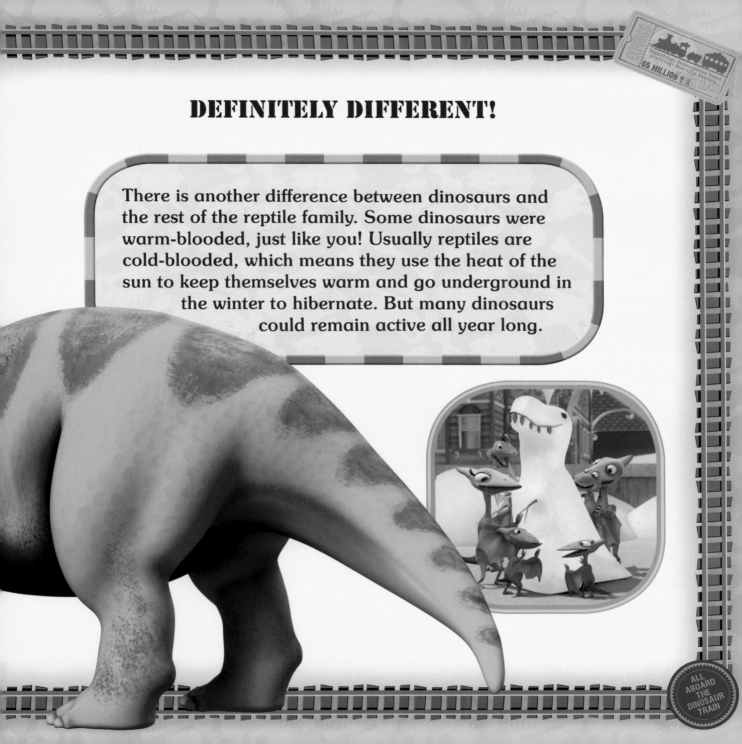

ALL ABOARD THE DINOSAUR TRAIN

PROFESSION: PALEONTOLOGIST

We know so much about dinosaurs thanks to the work of scientists called paleontologists. Like detectives, they look for clues, such as bones, teeth, claws, and footprints in the ground.

Let's take a look at this skeleton and figure out which dinosaur family it belonged to. Time to investigate!

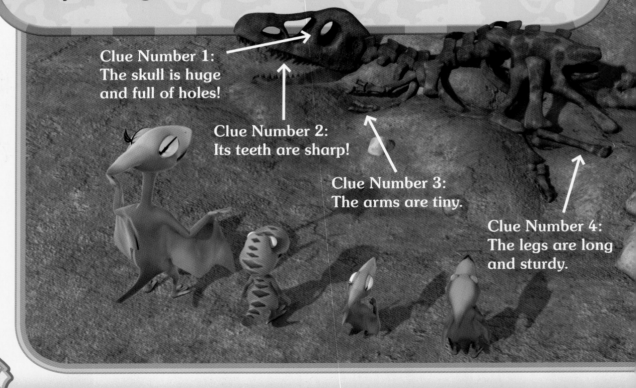

Clue Number 1:
The skull is huge and full of holes!

Clue Number 2:
Its teeth are sharp!

Clue Number 3:
The arms are tiny.

Clue Number 4:
The legs are long and sturdy.

THE DETECTIVE'S CONCLUSION

Big skull + sharp teeth + tiny arms + sturdy legs + long tail = theropod! Dinosaurs from this family were bipeds, meaning they walked on their hind legs. Their teeth were sharp, so they could eat meat! And their long tail helped them to keep their balance while running.

Clue Number 5:
Its tail is very long!

THE DINOSAURS OF THE TRIASSIC PERIOD

The Triassic period extended from 250 to 200 million years ago. The climate was hot and dry in most places. Desert stretched out almost everywhere. But who (or what) was living in such harsh conditions? To answer this question, let's get aboard the Dinosaur Train!

DESTINATION: EORAPTOR RAVINE!

The first dinosaurs appeared during the Triassic period. Back then, almost all of them resembled Erma Eoraptor, one of the oldest dinosaurs! Erma is very small and walks upright on her hind legs, with her long tail helping to keep her balance. She runs really fast! She is a carnivore (meat eater) and hunts little reptiles, insects, and small animals that are no larger than mice.

HI, PAULINE!

Pauline Proganochelys also lives during the Triassic period. Her tail is the shape of a club, and although she looks like a modern-day turtle, she isn't able to retract her head under her shell.

ALL ABOARD THE DINOSAUR TRAIN

DESTINATION: LESOTHOSAURUS LANDING!

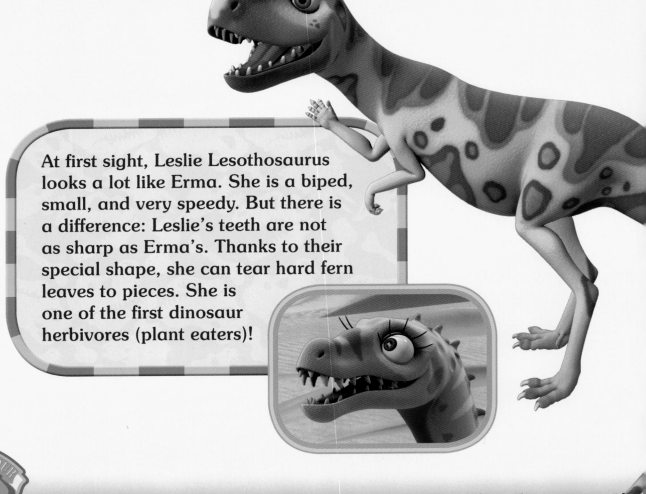

At first sight, Leslie Lesothosaurus looks a lot like Erma. She is a biped, small, and very speedy. But there is a difference: Leslie's teeth are not as sharp as Erma's. Thanks to their special shape, she can tear hard fern leaves to pieces. She is one of the first dinosaur herbivores (plant eaters)!

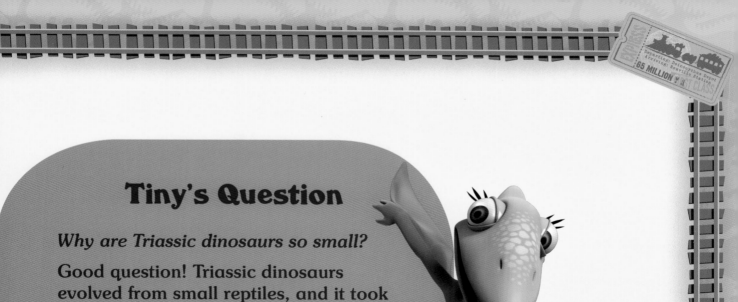

Tiny's Question

Why are Triassic dinosaurs so small?

Good question! Triassic dinosaurs evolved from small reptiles, and it took a long time for them to grow. One of the first big Triassic dinosaurs was the Plateosaurus. It was nearly thirty feet long. Its big neck grew longer, so it could reach the treetops where the leaves were!

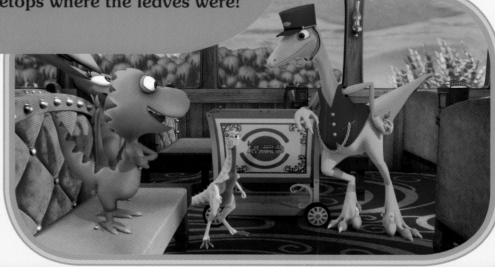

ALL ABOARD THE DINOSAUR TRAIN

THE DINOSAURS OF THE JURASSIC PERIOD

The Jurassic period was still very hot and much more humid. The climate was tropical, and enormous plants grew everywhere. This period, which extended from 200 to 145 million years ago, was known as the "Age of the Giants." Let's go for an expedition in the jungle!

This is Mr. Brachiosaurus. He lives with his wife and son, Ned, in a herd. They belong to the family of sauropods, the giant plant eaters of the Jurassic period. They have very long necks that allow them to reach treetop leaves.

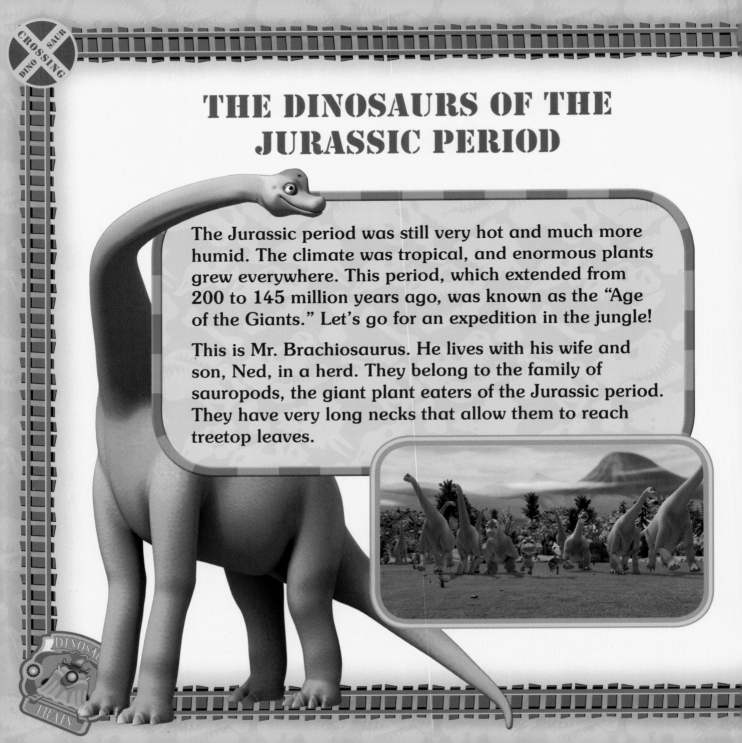

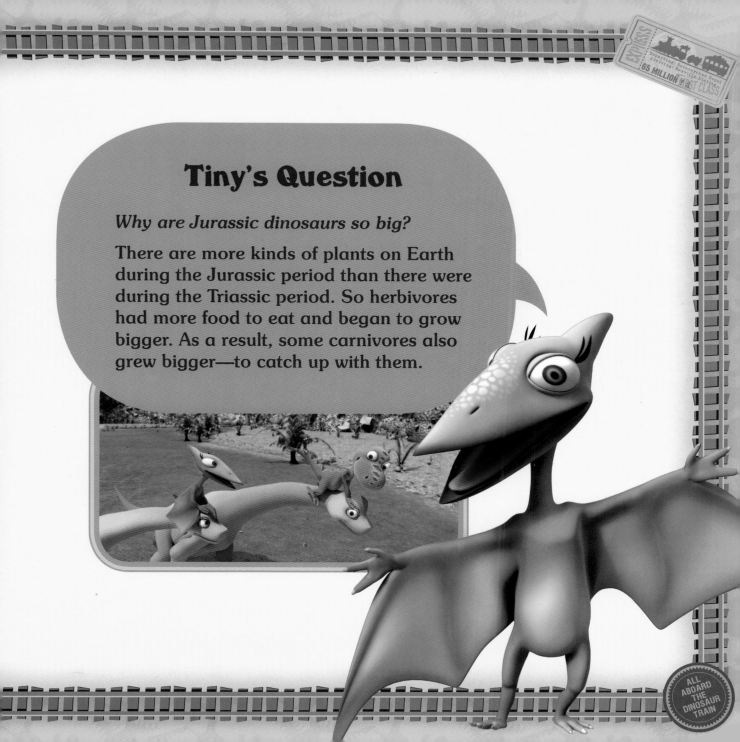

Tiny's Question

Why are Jurassic dinosaurs so big?

There are more kinds of plants on Earth during the Jurassic period than there were during the Triassic period. So herbivores had more food to eat and began to grow bigger. As a result, some carnivores also grew bigger—to catch up with them.

Alvin Allosaurus belongs to another dinosaur family: the meat-eating theropods. Alvin is huge, and he stands upright on his hind legs, like his ancestor Erma Eoraptor. His legs are muscular, and his arms are larger than Erma's. Alvin catches his prey by using his jaws full of sharp teeth.

This is Kenny Kentrosaurus. He is a plant eater who walks on four legs. He has a beak at the end of his mouth and funny plates on his body! What do you think they are used for?

Buddy's Hypothesis

I think these plates are used for different things. First, to scare carnivores because they are very impressive! He can also use them to cool himself down because it's stifling hot in the Jurassic period.

THE DINOSAURS OF THE CRETACEOUS PERIOD

We just traveled through the Time Tunnel and are now in the Cretaceous period, which extended from 145 to 65 million years ago! Dinosaurs lived all over the planet.

SOUTH AMERICA

Mr. Argentinosaurus is the giant of the giants, the biggest animal to ever live on land! He is over one hundred feet long and weighs one hundred tons. That's the weight of fourteen hundred humans!

NORTH AMERICA

Cory Corythosaurus is one of the Cretaceous period's many plant-eating dinosaurs. She has a duck-like beak and a funny crest on her head. She uses it to communicate with her family.

Keenan Chirostenotes also lives in North America. He has a toothless beak and big, agile legs. He eats lizards and small mammals that he hunts by running very fast. He also has claws and long arms with feathers on them, but he can't fly!

NEIGHBORS

Some of Cory and Keenan's neighbors include Hank Ankylosaurus, who has armor on his back, and Delores Tyrannosaurus, who has sharp teeth to help her eat meat!

BUDDY INVESTIGATES

Why are there so many different
dinosaurs during the Cretaceous period?

- Different species of dinosaurs
  developed on each continent.

- The climate was milder than during the Jurassic and Triassic periods. Ferns grew on the ground, and plants with flowers started to appear.
- New kinds of insects, mammals, and lizards appeared—along with new kinds of mammals who hunted them, like Cindy Cimolestes!

THE HERBIVORES

Many dinosaurs were herbivorous, which means they ate only plants. But they didn't all eat the same kinds of plants. Let's find out about these vegetarians.

THE TREETOP GRAZERS

Mr. Argentinosaurus loves eating treetop leaves. Like most long-necked dinosaurs, he has a small head (compared to the size of his body) and can easily reach high tree branches. His teeth are very thin and are all located in the front of his jaws. Do you know why?

Buddy's Hypothesis

To eat, the long-necked dinosaurs wrap their teeth around a branch and pull, so it helps to have all their teeth at the front of their mouths. The thin teeth tear off all the leaves, leaving a bare branch.

Tank Triceratops walks with his head close to the ground to gobble up everything that crosses his path: grass, ferns, and even bushes. His mouth is shaped like the beak of a parrot and is very sharp.

THE LAWN MOWERS

THE GOURMETS

Mrs. Lambeosaurus is more of a picky eater and loves scented flowers. Her curved neck allows her to graze on bushes, and despite her weight, she can also stand upright on her hind legs to reach the trees' tender leaves. She delicately picks them off the branches with her duckbill mouth.

THE CARNIVORES

Meat-eating dinosaurs belong to the theropod family. Buddy has gathered all of his cousins. Let's meet them!

Laura Giganotosaurus is the biggest in the family. She is twelve feet tall and as long as three cars lined up! Laura likes to hide and surprise her prey since it's less tiring than chasing after them!

A GIANT COUSIN

WHAT A GOOD NOSE!

Delores Tyrannosaurus has a very good sense of smell. She can smell prey from over half a mile away. When she attacks, she picks up her victim with her huge mouth.

BY THE WATER

Old Spinosaurus eats mostly fish. His head is long and thin, and his mouth is full of pointy teeth. He also has sharp claws to catch fish by swatting the water.

SHOW US YOUR TEETH, BUDDY!

Like every T. rex, Buddy has sixty teeth. These are the teeth of a carnivore! If Buddy breaks a tooth, a new one will grow to replace it.

IN THE AIR

Back in the days of dinosaurs, the sky was full of many different creatures. Who were they?

FIRST STOP: THE PTEROSAUR FLYING CLUB!

Pterosaurs had wings of skin, just like bats. They also had a bony tail, claws, and five-toed feet. They weren't birds because they didn't have feathers. They were flying reptiles! They flew up into the sky by flapping their wings and then glided, letting the wind carry them.

MR. PETEINOSAURUS

He is one of the first Pterosaurs. He has a long tail, like his land reptile ancestors. His large, toothed beak allows him to swallow insects while flying.

When Tiny is grown up, she will be nearly thirty feet wide when her wings are fully spread out.

TINY PTERANODON

QUINCY QUETZALCOATLUS

He is one of the biggest of the Pterosaurs. When he spreads his wings, he is almost forty feet wide!

SECOND STOP: THE MICRORAPTOR MOUNTAIN

Although Mikey Microraptor has feathers all over his body, he is like Buddy in many ways. He has the same tail, the same feet, and the same kind of arms. Mikey is a theropod dinosaur! Mikey's feathers let him fall slowly from the trees, but he is unable to fly!

LAST STOP: THE CONFUCIUSORNIS GARDENS

Chung Confuciusornis can really fly! Instead of a long, bony tail, he has two long feathers. Chung is one of the first true birds that ever lived on Earth.

UNDER THE SEA

Even though dinosaurs couldn't swim, it didn't mean the oceans were empty. They were full of animals. Let's take a closer look at them.

Elmer Elasmosaurus has a long neck and four paddle-shaped flippers. He has a small head, so he eats only tiny fish and shrimps. To catch them, he swims with his mouth open and then closes it. His teeth fit together to prevent his prey from coming out, and he swallows them whole.

Tiny's Question

Is Elmer a fish?

No, Elmer is a marine reptile. He breathes in the open air, coming up to the surface to catch his breath. If you look closer, you will notice small holes under his eyes; those are his nostrils.

FUNNY CREATURES!

Meet the Michelinoceras brothers! They are ammonites, the octopus's cousins. Their soft bodies are covered by shells. With their tentacles, ammonites catch fish and then crunch them with their beaks.

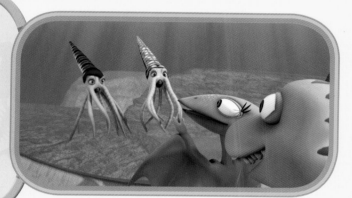

HI, CRAIG AND CARLA!

Craig and Carla Cretoxyrhina are sharks! Sharks, along with crabs, jellyfish, hermit crabs, shrimps, and corals, existed before the dinosaurs.

DINOSAUR RECORDS!

THE BIGGEST!

The Argentinosaurus was nearly one hundred feet long (the equivalent of one and a half tennis courts!) and weighed nearly one hundred tons (as much as ten African elephants).

THE TINIEST!

Without its long tail, the Microraptor would only be a little over seven inches high (the same size as a sparrow)!

THE SMARTEST!

Compared to its weight, the Troodon had the biggest brain of all the dinosaurs.

THE FASTEST!

The Ornithomimus dashed like a rocket with its long legs. Paleontologists estimate it could hit speeds close to fifty miles per hour. It was almost as fast as a cheetah, which runs at fifty-five miles per hour.

3. Who can walk on his or her hind legs?

Ned
Brachiosaurus

Leslie
Lesothosaurus

Arnie
Argentinosaurus

Kenny
Kentrosaurus

Pauline
Proganochelys

SEE YOU SOON ON THE DINOSAUR TRAIN!

Answers: 1. Tank Triceratops, 2. Erma Eoraptor,
3. Leslie Lesothosaurus